SHE IS ME

WRITTEN BY ADRIANA SPEARS   ILLUSTRATED BY BETHANY EVELYN

To order additional copies of this book, contact:
Xlibris
844-714-8691
www.Xlibris.com
Orders@Xlibris.com

ISBN: Softcover   978-1-6641-7341-5
        EBook   978-1-6641-7334-7

Print information available on the last page

Rev. date: 05/05/2021

SHE IS ME

She is so fun to be around.

We laugh...

play,

play,

She does my make-up

and paints my nails too.

She has the same skin complexion
as me maybe off a shade or two.

She has freckles on her face just like me.

When we wake we both have thick big puffy hair.

She combs and brushes my hair.

Now I'm off to school;

"Oh, cant forget
my glasses!"

I kiss and hug my baby sisters goodbye
because that's what big sisters do.

Printed in the United States
by Baker & Taylor Publisher Services